THE SUB-AMERICAN DREAM

JASON L. FORD

Cover Art designed by JLF

Photography by Joseph Henderson

Contributing Author - Krystal Nikol

ISBN: 978-0-578-42115-5

In memory of DeAngelo Barnell Snow

My brother and best friend

Table of Contents

The Big Bang

Welcome

Welcome Welcome

Recognize that even though I'm a guest

such would not exist

as I persist to God my mind without rest,

no one's contest.

My mind's compressed

beyond the length of its time,

Take the world to paint the Universe in simple designs.

It's me!

That "Brother", His "Mans", My "Nigga"!

Whatever you like, from day to the night

I brought the light, the dark, the future

despite the present.

All around us

light years through this space.

Look at the past ahead of us that we have yet to engage.

In the beginning

it was dense, depths were deep.

The stories told of white painting black

to define the light from the dark

until the collection of matters,

pillars of life

birthed stars by far the most amazing events that's never been seen.

They didn't know how real.

They never been that close to the sun.

With futile attempts to measure watts…

son since elementary,

my dear pen-pal, to reach that unrelatable space.

The truth.

The dense dark consumes the light.

Engulfs all that it's known; all that it could ever be.

But ignorance praises naivety.

It fly's fake love,

light doves,

overhead washed with white rags,

white flags.

And then

God, the dark graviton

pressure, pushing

forming the world that you see.

So, I guess we can say that you're blessed.

Now

with tears rolling, joining hands

in sorrow from the talk around being a vegetable.

Let's talk about being a vegetable.

Forced to wait on our blessings

pairing my pure emotion

with antibodies, peeling away with this knife.

But from the clouds, it's like a dream

forced being fed through a tube.

Even when the sun shines on my face

it casts a shadow behind me.

Within my ears, climbing up my skin

resting beneath the lids of my eyes. Senseless,

bathing.

Rejoice, the light from the dark.

So distracted by our issues presented to us

gift wrapped with rainbow ribbons and green paper that's littered

with micro-messages just to give us a cause.

Ignore distractions.

In order to expand, we must first understand.

To understand is to infer from information received.

Digest, consume for nutrition, not to wallow in waste.

Don't make sense of what does not but

all concepts have their place.

Currently, I understand that we can be distracted

by the things that we've learn to understand.

Justify that flashing light second to September.

That subpolar, bi-polar, sense.

Your desires acquired,

fire.

Ignore your design, dangle higher

as you attend with attire.

Changed clothes,

plain souls to new poles just to define your rotation

At a loss for words?

I've never lost my will to define.

So don't get lost. Unable to find one's way,

unknowing of one's whereabouts.

Just think.

Direct one's mind toward something.

Use one's mind actively to form connected ideas.

That instant touch above the clouds,

the beauty of celestial patterns.

That connection from me to you,

to you,

it's heavy it's deep.

It shakes the churches,

makes the people want to shout and stand to their feet.

Ah, maybe that weight is necessary for us to conquer our feats.

Maybe that weight is necessary for us to conquer our feats.

M1

My name is Jason L. Ford and this is The Sub-American Dream. This presentation is meant to be a journey, of sorts. A journey that is intended to provide the opportunity to engage various perspectives. Perspectives that even though they are similar in their origin show great variation due to the difference in experiences and their effects on our conditioning as social beings.

It is abstract, in the mind, the things that we go through in our pursuit of the American Dream. It is my hope that throughout this experience you will witness my personal growth. Furthermore, I hope that throughout you experience some growth of your own.

These words were not constructed to give all the answers, but to provide us with questions as we pursue our truths. Now, as we begin this journey, who here is familiar with "The American Dream"?

The American Dream (ideology) – is a national ethos of the United States. The set of ideals (democracy, rights, opportunity, liberty, and equality) in which freedom includes opportunity for prosperity and success, as well as, upward mobility for the family and children achieved through hard work in society with few barriers.

Now I would like to believe the statement. I do believe those opportunities for prosperity and success exist, but I find contention with that "few barriers" part.

We the People

Why are they so smart and we so stupid.

Clueless while they screw us.

Exclude us from what they call,

progression.

Properly investing not only dollar signs but steady time

droning minds.

All that shit in politics, feeds the rich steak dinners

while *we the people* lie dismembered

because we had just enough to quite someone else's stomach.

Meanwhile.

It's like everyday United Way finds a way to lose funds.

Cutting just enough off of the top

so no one would make them stop robbing the people.

I just wanna walk up to the foundation of Feed the Children

And tell them to just feed the fucking children.

Please feed our children.

Because my fathers donation

should be used to erase the screams of an unneeded pancreas.

Instead of replacing Audis with Benz's.

Like they had some sort of vengeance.

Like…

What did the kids ever do to them?

What did the people do to be fucked by Katrina

which brought a prostitute named FEMA

that eventually fucked the whole United States!

Federal Emergency Management Aid?!

In those moments FEMA should stood for…

Fuck Every that Makes America!

Fuck Freedom! Fuck Equality! Fuck everything!

We the People?

What people!?

Us People still stand divided and unequal.

and not only black and white but

kings and pawns.

and pawns kill pawns for kings

with no seen communication.

It's supposed to be We the Nation?

It seems we the People have no place in the nation in which we live.

Because this place wasn't designed for people.

It should be more like... We the Slaves...

"The Sub-American Dream."

Sub-, is a prefix with the meaning of, under, below, beneath, slightly imperfect, nearly, or secondary. A subcontinent is a large and distinctive portion of some continent. Substandard is a standard slightly imperfect when compared to the usual or required standard. Thus, Sub-American is a large, distinctive group of Americans whose existence has been disrupted and disjointed by the belief that they are secondary to other Americans.

"The Sub- American Dream" (ideology) - is a set of ideals in which freedom includes secondary opportunity for prosperity beneath ultimate success, as well as slight mobility for generations achieved through hard work in an imperfect society with many barriers.

As people, we are often taught or conditioned to believe that we are simply, not, good enough. That applies to all people and not those considered the minority. As those considered minorities, this country's forefathers have made us, the Sub-American, to internalize levels of inferiority about our own people, which reflects ultimately how we see ourselves. In an attempt to attain some kind of equal footing, we feel that we can excel best by beating someone else. We find satisfaction pursuing our goals believing that our success is predicated upon someone else's failure, breeding eco-systems filled with contempt and hate. We learn through our experiences. Often we are told by our idols to incentivize hate, and to be weary of love.

Personally, I would rather be a beacon of love, especially as a young man, a Black man. As an adolescent I used to write "love" on everything! I used to draw hearts on my notebooks, during my work breaks, only because I wanted everyone to believe in love. I wanted everyone to notice how important Love was. How important Love is. I even still find it difficult to write the word "Love" in lowercase because of my belief in its divine power. God is Love. Love is God.

But, one day, I found struggle: life's struggles. I found struggle like what you may know or have known, what you may be experiencing now. Struggles that accompany thoughts of how much it going to costs and when is it going to be past due.

In that struggle, I felt hate become me. I could feel the hate growing inside of me. For everything positive that I noticed, there was some level of hate projected; some level of "She got this, but ain't got that" and "He did this but can't do that". Taking a moment to think on why those emotions lingered so close, I realized that the hate I felt was a reflection of my personal disappointments. At that moment, that point of realization, I knew that I could understand hate on a new level.

The Idle Mind

Blank thoughts and idle time,

idle thoughts.

Idle thoughts lead to pipe bombs and great inventions.

Great intentions and false intuition bring disappointment

losing sheep feeding wolves.

Great disappointment on the hurder of the flock

allowing blank thoughts to become fed wolves counting sheep in

sweet dreams,

those itis dreams full of sheep.

How do we plan to live when everyone likes to follow the leader

and all the great leaders refuse to lead?

the story of my life

My story has the pages rearranged

because only with effort will you learn and understand,

learn to understand.

I sit in the light in the dark.

Blank thoughts and idle time burned my great inventions.

Results of disappointment or maybe the fear there of.

But owning "no fear of nothing", leaving the shelf sold out.

I hold out because failure stock fear bringing lost time

that could have been found.

But idle time heads nowhere fast.

Maybe I'm dreaming, counting sheep that helps me sleep after

dinner.

Afraid of wolves leading sheep to frontiers with no good intentions.

Bringing home, the bacon with the slaughter of their life's stock.

Forcing idle thoughts that were meant to be great inventions

to turn into pipe bombs and false intuition.

Self-demolition brings fed wolves and dead sheep.

Sleep wolves

while the blood creeps in the blank thoughts of the hurder of the

flock

in turn refusing to lead.

Great disappointment allowing great inventions to become pipe

bombs

wondering in idle thoughts,

What do wolves eat when there's no more sheep?

M3

When considering our current climate as it pertains to gender relations, what comes to mind?

I like to believe that it is our differences on the verge of bringing us closer together. Maybe that's wishful thinking. You may consider that, when looking around, things "just ain't what they used to be back in the days". The elders say that we live in neighborhoods, but are lacking community. Some want to incite fear. Promote the narrative that this is the beginning of the end of society as we know it!

I believe that there's maybe something positive in all of this. I believe that in times like these, of perceived discourse and honest debate, we arrive at a new state of awareness. Not only awareness of others, how others perceive or feel on a daily basis, but awareness of ourselves as well. There is the birth of a mutual respect via conversations regarding personal comfort.

If we take a quick look, we find that as living beings the things that we are less aware of have a greater chance to hurt us, to take advantage of us. Notice I said as living beings and not just human beings. And this is not a ploy for veganism. I just want you to consider this.

If you were unaware that you had a peanut allergy, there would be a higher probability of you being killed by a Snicker's bar. If one happened to discover a pond, one that you were unaware contains poisonous bacteria or feces; and was dying for a drink. Then there you might meet your ultimate fate taking that drink or simply by taking a bath.

If you're sexually active and unaware of your HIV status, you may not have the opportunity to live the full life you've planned. A life made possible by a proper diagnosis and with proper care. Without accessibility to sufficient healthcare, then death could be a result of an illness that could have been easily cured. Though I know I may be overdoing it, the message shouldn't be lost. For as it seems, the things that we are unaware of have the advantage over us, they have the greater ability to harm us.

Confidence is Queen

Beauty in the eye of a hurricane.

Behold the beauty of boldness,

the untimed essence of ebony.

Birthed of an addiction, the world,

pre-introduced to the trees and the sky.

The world as we know it.

Its eternal imminence

a product of disaster and phenom.

It's beyond,

flawless.

The question is,

what do you see when you look in the mirror?

Peering to what appears to just appeal to the eye.

But the truth is

that you're the heal to our cries,

and even from afar we salivate to possess some time in your arms.

As a woman, just being you

you are as beautiful as the sun.

What shine is blinding to eyes

but what is felt is so distinguished that it can't be trapped in the sky.

Raining reunions so missed

its like introductions, of

Love and inspiration.

Applauding strength for embracing something as heavy as you

but for Nefertiti it's too easy reppin' yourself.

As long as you're not too busy Keeping Up with the kardashians

to realize

in real lives real eyes are far ahead of the curves.

Even Marion learned,

losing her greatest achievement because

she didn't have faith

she could win.

See, building your fate knowing your place,

knowing your face is far more promising than any mask

stack up on made up foundation.

And nothing is scarier than being in hollows eve,

the creation of the world within sin,

the building of pain and insecurities.

See there is no security in depending on a blanket in a cold world

whose biggest interest in a cold girl is on her back side,

back slide into

wasted thoughts on 4 D's, reporting disappointment

dictating finals on undiscussed midterms.

Knowing it would be much smarter to invest interest into what

collects interest with time.

Puzzled on how many different sides

so many different colors,

mood rings complex creatures properly unexplained to the inferior

impatience.

See your inheritance is truly jeweled crowns

not gold rings and to be polished plastic on a mantle

is no accomplishment for no Queen.

Because a victorious Queen can still queen without Kings.

A glorious Queen.

Not a Queen to be,

unless Queen to be... noticed, by you.

So rather, Queen to see her blessing to be the blessing of life.

Because confidence is your most beautiful asset,

From,

Your Most Humble of Knights.

M4

These conversations about our individual levels of comfortable seem to make us more aware of ourselves. Sometimes we are more ignorant than unaware. I can relate because I am human. I have gone through with many things that did not necessarily make me feel comfortable. And this is common within our society. Why? Perhaps we just want to fit in. To hide in plain sight? To have friends that "accepts" us. Most don't consider the fact that if change is required for our acceptance then we weren't truly accepted at all. We are actually accepting the simple truth that our "friends"/peers do not approve of us as we are.

To step out, to be different a lot of people will attribute to courage. To be courageous. Courage - (n) the quality of mind or spirit that enables a person to face difficulty, danger, pain, etc. without fear. Difficulty, danger, pain? I can't help but to wonder, where is the danger in wanting to stay home and doing some studying instead going out the day before the test? What is difficult about not doing something that you aren't comfortable doing? What's painful about not wanting to spend your night somewhere that doesn't feel like home? What is there to fear?

Are we aware of those fears at all? Are we aware? As we live in fear everyday, I as a black / Afro-American male am not able to own up to my fears. As African American males we cannot show that we have fears, even when they exist. We can confess to fears that are general, perhaps fears that are universal within our community, even if they're not personal fears of our own. Maybe that's just one of the ways that we try to fit in.

Go out and ask a black man about the things that he fears, and he might say the police. Rightfully so. Generally. But never to express any fear of death, or heartbreak, or of another man who isn't wearing a badge and a gun simultaneously with a false sense of authority.

But the truth is that we all possess fears, very real fears that we feel would be remiss to express or even acknowledge as we develop as individuals. We could never express our fears those vulnerabilities. That's maybe because of the fear that someone might attempt to "capitalize" on our vulnerabilities. Because of the fact that we could never express our fears, we never actually realized them. We are less aware of our fears.

Remember the things we are less aware of are the biggest threat to our wellbeing.

Brand New Sentiment

Brand new sentiment.

Wash those old drawers with fresh blood

to stain windows

to remove the feelings of motionless glass.

The emotion in the sick mind

the sad patient waiting to break free from the inevitable jacket.

Undeniably matching the hats.

Got to get people to click clique clique click…

follow so I don't feel failure walking off this roof to my demise.

Losing my life to my brain shaking from the impact of death.

Cement rising 6 feet

result of the weight of my sins.

Taking note to my tears etched in the sidewalks and their books,

for life, like manuals.

Handle actuals, or…or actually,

you have never seen success to a standard.

Flattered failure with class, in class,

but I passed the flying colors to going mothers birthing new

expressions

for fathers disregarding the truth to sleep lies.

To close eyes without wet dreams, cold sweats,

a cold death to family.

Buy Ohana with the dollars printed on the back of their necks.

Balance reading the accounts of dead dreams.

Living in nightmare fantasies.

Those dream's cast Sega's Saturns trapping the free in boxes.

Handcuff you in basements until it makes you want to play the game.

And embrace the rain until we realize the sun actually exists

after following ignorance like drunk moths before crashing into every

artificial hour.

Until the fall of the moon.

Open my eyes right before the end floating high on the tide.

Watching the empty hopes of my broken promises drift away with the night.

Salvation from a moment clear and peers through the shade.

Feeling my nightmares hiding in the shadows taking advantages to my mistakes.

Closed the door to back massages, private jets, pride the jet clouds dense with disadvantages.

Dense with thoughts that circle to keep my mind on its feet.

Heavy is freedom, expend the truth in the land of the free.

A concept that I want to be sure to address is "privilege". Privilege – (n) a right, immunity to consequence, or benefit enjoyed only by a person beyond the advantages of most.

Privilege plays a big role in "The American Dream", but it plays a more integral role in "The SubAmerican Dream". Recently, I had a conversation with a group of my peers; family, friends…and we concluded that privilege is not limited to race. If I may, I'll start at the top.

In the United States, from the early 1600s through 2018- I mean, 1865, there was what is called institutionalized slavery. Contrary to what is often taught, Nat Turner was not alone in his fight for human rights. Many of the people enslaved within this system aspired to be free. They took steps to plan and execute their escape from captivity. There were even private meetings held with the objective of developing and organizing what we would now fit into the definition of revolution.

Many of the enslaved people just wanted to survive. They did what was expected, what was necessary in order to witness another sunrise and withstand another sunset.

In those times, times of much turmoil and degradation, developed many different coping mechanisms for the displacement. For some, coping meant accepting their role in society. Along with acceptance came the desire to gain a position of privilege within the system. They provided information to the slave owner about the plans of the enslaved. They even, in some instances, assisted in the hunt, capture, and murder of folks that were of their own kin.

In today's society we have arrived in a new state of being, a new sense of freedom, a new kind of slavery. In order to preserve privilege, slavery has metamorphosized into a system that though it is inextricably linked to race, includes socioeconomic status and gender and religion and nationality and education...

As some of us went to a university for opportunity and worked hard to get our job, earning our $45,000 to enjoy our newfound "privilege". We find it hard to accept that a person who went to technical college, or God forbid, no college at all, could earn as much as we do because of the possibility of it diminishing our privilege. We enjoy that feeling of privilege; which is probably similar to the privilege our bosses and executives feel when we are at "the office".

We want the privilege associated with that level of success. We want the new fashion or the new shoes; we don't care what they look like, we just care what it costs. We care that we can afford it, or that we can make others believe that we can afford it. We want others to look at us and see it, smell it when we walk through a room. "That person seems to have more than me so that person must be more than I am".

One of the biggest issues with privilege is that it creates gaps in the information that we receive and transmit. It shelters us in an ecosystem that is ruled by the material things acquired and the things we desire. Trapping those that are perceived to be free in boxes.

People cannot achieve what they don't know is real, what they don't see as achievable, when they are naïve to its existence in reality.

Today/Tomorrow

I want your attention!

I mean, I need you to listen.

You even made a living the route I've been giving so I could receive

your position.

Toting the front line good and ridden just to play second fiddle.

Only God knows what I'm given so don't be quick to belittle.

Inside my love ones I realize pain of beloved drugs

to belong and to be loved once by this world of deterred sons.

But honestly in my universe.

Aligned stars are by far beyond hard to believe.

Beyond far, impalpable a cold fish in the sea.

That's the youth's anthem without banter from the world's fair.

The world's glare shines out our vision, we don't even recognize our

own stare.

And nowadays we're estranged alternative to reality famed and

framed in brass rubbish justified by technicalities.

We have trust issue within our love,

in hate we find our comfort, afraid to claim our greatness,

because failure sleeps in our comfort a bed we find our fate in.

Failed to be flesh, not fresh.

To be fly!

The holy word such gravity,

those angel wings we defy.

Truth is,

everybody's at the table with themselves in the center.

Nobody wants to listen without their points to deliver.

Everybody wants the bag, possess to have,

and make a living which makes the living a nest of sorrows

dead hallows of said giving.

And I'm a victim too!

Suspect the proof lest my deliverance.

I done gave just to take the mirror shades the real resemblance.

Swept in the wave to lose my name achieve some fame attained in dissonance.

Became a slave of day to day waiting for death but in my self-defense.

Listen, I said listen, the kids need your attention.

They need real Love and guidance not your self-inflating permission.

And really what so amazing..., I mean I'm just so amazed in today.

How we walk pass ones we Love and speak not a word or a phrase.

Offer nothing not a murmur, nothing of praise nor disgrace.

But get on that phone, Twitter, Facebook, and have so much to say.

And then we rock proud colors like we're brothers in blood.

Tales from the crypt seen sisters trip over luster and love.

Turn our backs to show our age in maturation.

Imagine nation's true ability

if we wasn't so divided undecided in futility.

So, listen to each other find yourself in the litter.

Only you've got what your given so don't be quick to belittle.

Be benign behind sights, be hindsight for the kids.

Your experiences bring opportunity for others to live.

And you might reveal that purpose that you're looking to find.

In your might, reseal that purpose that you're living to bind.

Within Life, a civil circle to uplift in divine.

Center self in hurricanes that you can look in the eye.

M6

It is rarely publicized, the contributions of the Sub-American to our society. Many people don't know that it was Richard Spikes an African American who invented the automatic gear shift, the turn signal, and the beer tapper amongst other things. Or Guillermo Gonzalez, a Cuban American responsible for our being able to watch color images on television screens. Before the release of the film, "Hidden Figures", many Sub-Americans including myself didn't know about Katherine Johnson who was the African American woman whose skills and intellect were critical in successfully advancing the agenda of the United States to explore space. Many would not know to credit Fernando Torres, a Hispanic inventor, who invented the sim card the next time they are using their iPhone.

The unfortunate truth is that we often aspire to be, to have, what we have witnessed. What is tangible? If we don't know that it is possible for us to be the scientist that studies diseases to discovers an efficient cure for cancer or have never met anyone who has communicated with a person living/working in a space station, then we settle in our minds that those things are in faux fact impossible.

There are a few contributions by Sub-Americans that could never go unmentioned. One founded in my home State, Michigan. The first minority owned Fortune 500 Company. Black owned, Black funded, Black operated. Motown Records, a company that grew to change and influence the world in many ways.

The American Dream: Gordy's Glory

There was always something superstitious.

Very, very supernatural

how songs infested my mind.

Lyrics scripted, engraved relentless,

like the writing was on the walls.

Man… I could even catch the rhythm in the rise and the falls,

auto engine installs,

melodic heaven in the hell of it all.

Back in the days, through this window the looking glass

brass innuendo.

The benefit found in love that only a family provides.

A family born and bred in the city of motor vehicles,

so the story as its tread show the drive through trafficked intervals.

Quality controlled by a system process so visceral.

Assemble lines that were pivotal, steps to greatness was literal.

Educate the kids they don't wind up broke.

Begging for food,

while expression screaming money,

that's what I want.

Like please Mr. Postman I've been waiting for a miracle.

Shop around your first single because the last sounds what you're

living through.

Up at 3 in the morning trying to find a fast track.

To see a million but it's smoky still excited from the last pack.

And we were born to hustle,

flex the muscle indeed, but 9 to 5's not my speed.

The spirit of my father in me.

Maybe my potential is seen, in the potential of the ones who believe.

Planting the seed of purpose, surfaced the glows of the green.

Take the girls away from chores scrubbing on floor,

to open doors to platforms where supernovas are formed.

Divorce depression from oppression,

bye baby with the stressing.

Mar(r)y wells in bridal gowns running over spewing blessings.

So far removed that they can fine that comfortable grove on the back

of the bus,

until they rushed to the front cause bullets passed burst that shallow

bubble of trust.

To give them a lane to free that pain that we find hard to explain.

Because time in exchange in finding ways to fly with food on our

plates.

Print blacks on whites for the ages something ageless

rewrite history.

The magic man, Abraham, Martin kinged the crown of Kennedy.

Grandstand on bandstands, world conquerors like the British.

Navy blues come to review; you see the blues mix with the rhythm.

On high ground

sometimes I wonder if the Lord had played a prank on me.

Recording hoarding thoughts mimic rhythmic somatic symphonies.

As Barry Gordy, I bear the glory, but my family made it true.

Afterhours in the gyms tryna find them a grove.

You see their faces mixed and matched, the race to learn what is new.

The prophetic dropout keeping the kids in the schools.

Before I go, I want to provide a little background on myself. I was born in a small city called Saginaw, Michigan. A city whose fame, before Draymond Green seemed to be only found in acts of crime and murder. I grew up as a child with aspirations of changing the world. Aspirations of helping others realize their potential by attempting to decode for them the things that seemed hard for them to see. In truth, there were many things that I failed to realize for myself.

One of my closest childhood friends left home to find a better life for himself, to live the American Dream. We were more like brothers than friends, as I remember the plenty conversations we had after his deciding to join what was known as the "War on Terror".

On September 17, 2010 De'Angelo Barnell Snow was killed in Afghanistan when insurgents attacked his vehicle with a rocket-propelled grenade. At that time, I was 21 years old, approaching my senior year at Eastern Michigan University in pursuit of my idea of the American Dream.

Less than three years later, on March 3rd of 2013, a new universe was born. Queen Taylor Dion Ford came into the world healthy and happy. I was 23 years old, settling into post-graduation. For me my daughter had become a new perspective in life, a new nucleus for all living beings.

The Past, The Future

Cinematic setting with no actors in sight,

Rapper's Delight,

sugarcoat hills with thrills of the night.

Adrenaline fights to the death with the feeling of life.

Unprojected, finding protection from the weapons in spite.

Wrestle the knife.

Collide the avid theft of the life.

World full of hype.

Forced to shake people's lefts stead of rights.

Left full of spite.

Making you push what's left to the right.

Left with some rights, but rights ain't left us fit for the fight.

I remember the nights,

watching the block, hooping and all.

I remember the day, the terms, I had to hang your face on the wall.

I remember the mall. Remember the whips we'd grip when we ball?

Marble on walls

with diamond lining glass shower stalls.

I remember it all.

Fighting to live the dreams of the past.

Tall for a task, forced to bring it back to the future at last.

A historian,

pushing Deloreans from trash for a dash.

Seasoned from all four seasons, shaking stash for the cash.

In space, remember the day I first saw her beautiful face.

Angel of grace,

created by Gods the feeling to face.

The race, gotta outrun the force created in hate.

Deal with the pain, be the being to be in this state.

Don't fall into pace.

Be sure to value the time in the day.

Right now, within this minute

I take a second to state. Tomorrow in all its glory is a fictional place.

Today is dead babies, tomorrow's the excuse people make.

A thought that we exalt to bring a future to be,

but today will be determining the future you'll see.

Back to the time, seconds like hours that were ours to meet.

Sound full of sweet, broken down my empowered defeat.

Empowering present the God a heaven hardly beseeched.

Hard to just speak of all the colors dying to be.

Dying to breathe, to give life

Die to give the unseen.

Live the obscene.

The things you dream you'll learn to believe.

Queen Taylor Dion Ford

Spc. DeAngelo Barnell Snow

Roll Bounce by Joseph Henderson

Youngins by Joseph Henderson